NOVEN

TO

ST. BENEDICT

THE LITURGICAL PRESS
Collegeville, Minnesota 56321

Imprimi potest: John A. Eidenschink, O.S.B., J.C.D., Abbot of St. John's Abbey. *Nihil obstat:* William G. Heidt, O.S.B., *Censor deputatus. Imprimatur:* ✚ George H. Speltz, D.D., Bishop of St. Cloud, September 21, 1976.

ISBN 0-8146-0803-5

SAINT BENEDICT
(480 - 547 A.D.)

A novena of prayers or any other devotion in honor of a saint will be more meaningful if we first refresh our minds by recalling at least the main events of the saint's life. We offer these few notes on St. Benedict's life, so that those who use this novena may do so more intelligently, and understand more clearly what devotion to St. Benedict implies.

St. Benedict and his twin sister, St. Scholastica, were born of noble Roman parents in Norcia, Italy, seventy miles north-east of Rome, about the year 480 A.D. Four years earlier, in 476, the barbarian king Odoacer had captured the last Roman emperor and thus put an end to the Roman Empire of the West.

As a young man, perhaps at seventeen or eighteen years of age, Benedict was sent to Rome to complete his education, likely in philosophy and law, as was the custom for young men of noble families in those days. How long he remained in Rome, we do not know. He probably fled the city about 493, when Theodoric the Great, an Ostrogoth, overthrew Odoacer and established the Gothic rule over Italy (493-555). This covered the remaining span of St. Benedict's life. At any rate, Benedict decided that the political turmoil and the sinful pagan environment mixed with the influence of the Arians were not for him, what with Odoacer's barbarians first in control, and then the Arian rule of the Goths.

Everything around him seemed to militate against the Catholic training he had received from his parents in Norcia. Concerned about his eternal salvation and wanting nothing more than "to seek God," he fled Rome and took the road to Subiaco, a rocky, rugged region some thirty miles east of

Rome. Near Subiaco, he found a cave which seemed to fit his purpose: to live in silence and prayer.

He was not however completely isolated. There were shepherds in the vicinity and monks in some nearby monasteries. Upon meeting one of the monks, Romanus by name, the youthful Benedict confided to him his desire to live a life of prayer as a monk. Romanus, in his charity, provided Benedict with a monastic habit, and brought him food from time to time, lowering the food in a basket with a rope reaching down to the cave from the rocky ledge above. This went on for some three years.

Shepherds and neighboring monks eventually found out about the holy youth, and his fame as a "man of God" spread. Some of the monks from the nearby monastery at Vicovaro came and begged him that he be their abbot. Reluctantly, and to his later regret, he accepted. The monks soon rejected him because he would not yield to their lack of discipline. They tried to get rid of him by poisoning the wine he was about to drink at table. Seeing their bad will, Benedict went back to Subiaco where he eventually founded twelve small monasteries, each with twelve monks governed by an abbot. Benedict himself presided over one of them. This is where the two young men, Placid and Maur, were received into the monastery by St. Benedict.

However, in the course of his years at Subiaco, Benedict again met with opposition. The envy and harassment to which he was subjected finally prompted him to leave, taking with him Placid and Maur and a number of other companions, about the year 527 or 528. By this time he must have been about forty-eight years of age. With his companions he went to Monte Cassino, some seventy-five miles southeast of Rome, where he ruled as abbot for the rest of his life. That is how Monte Cassino became known as "the cradle of the Benedictine Order," although Benedict himself did not have in mind the founding of an Order, something unknown at the time.

His chief concern was to establish a community of monks at Monte Cassino, who would live together in the charity and peace of Christ "under a rule and an abbot," with the Gospel teachings of Christ as their guide.

His sister Scholastica had by this time established herself as a vowed virgin in a house or convent near the foot of Monte Cassino. Presumably she had a number of like-minded companion virgins with her, with whom she prayed and worked, and looked after the needs of the poor of the vicinity, especially the needs of sick and poor women and children. It was the custom for vowed virgins in those days to exercise such works of charity, besides living a community life of prayer and work, or even living in their parental home, yet publicly acknowledged and respected as vowed virgins.

It was at Monte Cassino that Benedict made a final copy of the Rule which bears his name, a rule which has been so universally admired for its wisdom and reasonableness that St. Benedict has been called the "Patriarch of Western Monks" ever since. He reorganized and improved the structure of monastic life and brought it to a high spiritual level, such as was not known before. There were many other monastic rules for monks and nuns at the time in the West, but the Rule of St. Benedict replaced them all, except the earlier and much briefer religious rule written by St. Augustine of Hippo in Africa (354-430).

That St. Benedict was truly "a man of God" is shown by St. Gregory the Great (540-604) in his Dialogs (II), where he not only sketches St. Benedict's life, but tells of some forty-two extraordinary events in the life of Benedict: miraculous cures, visions, prophecies, exorcisms, and raising a dead boy to life. That is why St. Benedict was already highly venerated during his earthly life both at Subiaco and at Monte Cassino. Monks, priests, and faithful laity came to him for spiritual guidance and asked for his prayers over them. Many brought the sick and disturbed to be cured by him, and the poor came to him for alms.

TWO FEASTS OF ST. BENEDICT. After Benedict's death, March 21, 547 (this is the date accepted by most scholars today), devotion to him was centered in the Mass and Liturgy of the Hours celebrated in his honor on March 21 each year. He has thus been chiefly honored for the past fourteen centuries.

But March 21 always falls during Lent, and this has had a restraining effect on the festive character of the day. The Holy See eventually decreed that a new feast, the Solemnity of St. Benedict, could be celebrated on July 11, honoring St. Benedict as the Patriarch of Western Monks. The feast of March 21 was retained to commemorate his death, so that Benedictines have had two feasts each year on which they honor their holy founder.

That is how matters stood for many centuries until Pope Paul VI (Oct. 21, 1964, AAS 56, 965) decreed that henceforth July 11 was to be kept in the Roman Calendar as the feast of St. Benedict to honor him as the chief heavenly Patron and Protector of Europe. By special decree, many monasteries and convents continue also to commemorate St. Benedict's death on March 21.

MEDAL OF ST. BENEDICT. A special form of devotion to St. Benedict is the wearing of the medal of St. Benedict. The earliest medal dates back to 1647. Since then, various forms of the medal have been struck, but the most widely accepted one to this day is the so-called Jubilee Medal of St. Benedict, which was designed and minted by the monks of Monte Cassino in 1880 to commemorate the 14th centenary celebration of the birth of St. Benedict (480-1880).

OBLATES OF ST. BENEDICT. Even before the medal of St. Benedict became popular, there were devoted followers of St. Benedict among the laity. There was St. Frances of Rome (1384-1440), born of a noble Roman family, gathering a group of Roman women together for the purpose of living a community life of prayer in so far as their state in life permitted. With the Rule of St. Benedict as their guide, they dedicated themselves and their wealth to the service of God and the welfare of the poor and needy, making promises, not vows, to live their life in accord with the spirit of the Rule of St. Benedict. Officially, they were called Oblates of St. Benedict.[1] They were the original Oblates of St. Benedict; namely, laity who affiliate themselves to a Benedictine monastery or convent, but live their life in the lay state, looking after the needs of their families, but over and above that, spending what time they can in prayer, and performing works of charity as the circumstances of their life allow and as the needs of the poor and the sick indicate.

To this day, there still are women Oblates in Rome, with their headquarters at the convent of Tor de' Specchi, but in the present century these Oblates of St. Frances of Rome have been making profession of vows, and live a complete convent life in Rome, helping the poor and the needy as they always have, in the spirit of St. Frances of Rome, with the Rule of St. Benedict as their guide, and are directly under the jurisdiction of the Holy See.

In some places, we have Oblates who live in the monastery or convent itself, observing the Rule in the same way as the monks or nuns. They do not make profession of vows, but make the same promises as other Oblates in the lay state. While living in the monastery or convent, these claustral Oblates, as they are called, are subject to the will of the superior in the same manner as the monks and nuns who make vows.

However, the vast majority of Oblates of St. Benedict today (and there are perhaps some 10,000 in the United States alone) are faithful lay people who, in their devotion to St.

[1] The word "oblate" is from the Latin word "offerre" which means to offer; and "oblate" therefore means one who is offered. Oblates are those who offer themselves to God.

Benedict, follow the Rule as their spiritual guide in so far as
their state in life and occupation or profession allow, spend
some extra time in prayer each day and do whatever good
works they can, especially for the needy and the poor. By their
very presence with others, and by their example of Christian
living, they become a special source of inspiration to others.
As lay Oblates of St. Benedict they have the same canonical
status as members of Third Orders, but they are not called a
Third Order because St. Benedict did not write a special Rule
for the laity. His Rule for monks is so easily understood and
adaptable to the life of the laity that there was no need for
another Rule. Diocesan priests are also accepted as Oblates.

A NOVENA OF PRAYER TO ST. BENEDICT. Most
of us are no doubt fascinated by the lives of great men and
women. This attraction extends no less to God's saints. Most
of us find ourselves drawn to one or more special saints, whose
lives inspire us, whose writings or charitable deeds spur us on
to be as courageous as they were to follow Christ. Thus, many
are singularly attracted to St. Benedict and his way of life, because of his humaneness and common sense in guiding us on
the way that leads to God, as described in his Rule for Monks.

Many of the laity read the Rule and find therein wise
guidance in solving many of the spiritual problems of life.
Others honor St. Benedict by having a medal of St. Benedict
about their person or in their homes. Others are so drawn to
St. Benedict's way of life that they ask to become Oblates of
St. Benedict. Finally, there are those many others who find
new spiritual strength by making a novena of prayer to St.
Benedict from time to time.

A novena is of course nine days of prayer. There are times
when we feel a great need for such prolonged prayer. But the
number nine is in itself quite arbitrary and does not of itself
offer any guarantee of special favors, any more than do the
numbers three, six, eight, twelve, thirteen, thirty, and so forth.

It is rather the daily or frequent repetition of our calling on God and His saints for help that increases our faith, hope, and charity, and thus helps to bring us into closer union with God, makes us more ready to do God's will rather than our own, and helps us better to see things from God's point of view rather than from our own.

Immersed in God's love we become strong in God, ready to accept the trials and hardships of life, but also ready to be grateful to God if He grants us any special favors or blessings, even blessings in disguise. We therefore pray for courage on the one hand, and for the ability to show our gratitude to God on the other, by living our life in accord with His will. We can then more easily identify ourselves with Christ and share His agony in the garden of Gethsemane, when he prayed to the Father with great anguish of soul: "Father, if it is your will, take this cup from me; yet not my will but yours be done" (Luke 22:42).

That is the spirit in which we should offer all our prayers to God. It is the spirit in which we should make a novena. It is the spirit of contentedly bowing to God's will without murmuring. It is the spirit suggested by our Lord, that we pray always, as we read in Luke: "Jesus told them a parable on the necessity of praying always and not losing heart" (18:1). The parable was about the corrupt judge who nonetheless yielded to the request of the widow who repeatedly demanded that her rights against an opponent be defended. The judge finally upheld her right because of her repeated insistence. Then, too, St. Paul writes to the Thessalonians: "Rejoice always; never cease praying; render constant thanks; such is God's will for you in Christ Jesus" (1 Thess. 6:16-18).

It is in this spirit that we offer this Novena to St. Benedict for all who are interested in St. Benedict. We are encouraged to do so by the teachings of Vatican Council II, which has the following to say about devotions, that is, non-liturgical prayers:

"Popular devotions of the Christian people, provided they conform to the laws and norms of the Church, are to be highly recommended, especially where they are ordered by the Apostolic See.

"Devotions proper to individual churches also have a special dignity if they are undertaken by order of the bishops according to customs or books lawfully approved. But such devotions should be so drawn up that they harmonize with the liturgical seasons, accord with the sacred liturgy, are in some way derived from it, and lead the people to it, since in fact the liturgy by its very nature is far superior to any of them" (*The Constitution on the Sacred Liturgy*, no. 13).

"Devotions which owe their origin to the customs or the laws of a locality or institute should be accorded reverence. Care should be taken, however, especially if they are performed in common, that they be in keeping with the liturgy, and that they take account of the liturgical seasons" (*Instruction on Proper Implementation of the Constitution on Sacred Liturgy*, SRC September 26, 1964, no. 17).

In accord with the above principle of Vatican II, the novena in this booklet is a revision of the Novena to St. Benedict which was composed by a monk of St. John's Abbey and first published in 1957, running through six printings since then. We hope that this new edition will open to admirers of St. Benedict some facets of his richly endowed character, and at the same time offer them a model for praising God in the manner St. Benedict so loved and stressed for the *Opus Dei*—the Work of God—in his directions for the Liturgy of the Hours: Hymn, Psalm, Reading, and Prayer. We recommend the novena for both public and private devotion at any time, but especially as a preparation for the two feasts of St. Benedict: March 21 and July 11, on the nine days preceding these feasts.

The Christianizing influence of St. Benedict's spirit upon the world has been duly acknowledged by historians and Popes, even in recent years; and the force of his monastic Rule as a guide for the spiritual life has been recognized by thousands of his sons and daughters and devoted clients through the centuries. In our own day, when the Order of St. Benedict is manifesting remarkable renewal, it is but natural that, with a better understanding of the life and spirit of St. Benedict, popular devotion to him would also flourish anew.

Through the intercession of St. Benedict, as he writes in his Rule, "let us prefer nothing whatever to Christ, and may He bring us all to everlasting life" (ch. 72).

St. John's Abbey
Collegeville, Minnesota
July 11, 1976

First Day

THE SAINT

A hymn introduces the Novena prayers each day; suggested melodies for singing this hymn are given on pages 39-40.

> The golden sun lights up the east,
> Recalls, by solemn yearly feast,
> When Benedict ascended high
> To heaven's mansions in the sky.
>
> O gracious father, on this day,
> With humble hearts and words we pray,
> That, taught by you to live aright,
> We may enjoy God's vision bright.
>
> All praise to God the Father be
> And to His Son, eternally;
> With equal glory, as is meet,
> To God the Holy Paraclete.

ANTIPHON: There was a man of venerable life, Benedict, blessed by God both in grace and in name.

PSALM 1. *The Good and the Wicked.*

How happy those who follow not the evil ways of wicked men: * they walk not in the ways of sin, / nor in the sinful company of irreligious, scornful men.

Their joy is in the law of God: * both day and night they think of it;

Like trees that grow by running streams and in due season yield their fruit; / like trees whose leaves are ever green and do not wither in the sun, * so they are blessed with happiness, / they find their fortune everywhere, / in all they undertake to do.

Not so the wicked who, like chaff, are blown about by every wind; * their cause at judgment will not stand, / nor will there be a place for them among the righteous and the just.

The Lord, indeed, protects the just who faithfully observe his law / and find their happiness therein; * but those who walk in sinful ways / will meet destruction in the end.

ANTIPHON:　There was a man of venerable life, Benedict, blessed by God both in grace and in name.

A READING FROM THE DIALOGS OF ST. GREGORY (II, Prol.).

There was a man, Benedict, who was revered for the holiness of his life, blessed by God both in grace and in name. While yet a boy, he showed mature understanding, and possessed a strength of character far beyond his years, keeping his heart detached from sinful worldly pleasures. While still in the world, he was in a position to enjoy all that the world had to offer; but, seeing how empty it was, he turned from it without regret.

Ŗ.　Thanks be to God.

Ꝟ.　The law of God is in his heart,

Ŗ.　And his steps do not falter.

PRAYER:　Let us pray. Almighty and eternal God, may the example of blessed Benedict urge us to strive for holiness of life and, by celebrating his memory, may we be inspired to follow him in the spirit of his Rule. This we ask of you through Christ our Lord.　Ŗ. Amen.

PRAYER FOR A HAPPY DEATH

Ꝟ.　Pray for us, holy Father Benedict.

Ŗ.　That we may obtain the grace of a happy death.

Holy Father Benedict, * blessed by God in grace and in name, * while standing in prayer with your hands raised to heaven, * you most happily yielded your angelic spirit into the hands of your Creator. You promised zealously to defend against the snares of the enemy, * in the last struggle of death, * those who shall daily remind you * of your glorious departure and your heavenly joys. Protect us therefore * this day and every day by your holy blessing, * that we may never be separated from our blessed Lord, * from the company of yourself and of all the blessed. We ask this through Christ our Lord.　Amen.

REFLECTIONS ON SEEKING GOD

The life of St. Benedict clearly marks the Christian way of life. The alert wayfarer will notice three important sign posts along the road.

I. SEEKING GOD.

The first is a whole-hearted seeking after God. St. Gregory impresses upon the reader of his Dialogs the one aim which determined St. Benedict's life from boyhood to old age, namely, to seek God and to glorify Him in all things. As a boy he left the pagan atmosphere of Rome to find God in the solitude of Subiaco. Thenceforth nothing could swerve him from the direct way to God.

II. UNCOMPROMISING DETACHMENT.

There must be no change of mind about the destination. What may lead us off the right course are the sinful attractions of the world. To escape their disastrous influences, we need not flee into solitude, but our hearts must not be unduly attached to persons and things on this earth. "No one can serve two masters" (Matthew 6:24). The hermit of Subiaco went the whole way of separation from earthly ties, and God blessed him the more abundantly with heavenly riches.

III. RESOLUTE PERSEVERANCE.

The struggle to overcome "the world, the lust of the flesh, and the lust of the eyes, and the pride of life" (1 John 2:16) is not easy. It demands all the strength of will that is in us, plus the special help of divine grace, to be victorious. The young Benedict met the crisis of temptation so resolutely that he remained thereafter undaunted and unrelenting in his quest for God. Perhaps we have too often adopted a compromising attitude and were caught in the meshes of sin. "If your hand or your foot cause you to sin, cut it off, and throw it from you" (Matthew 18:8).

Second Day

THE MONK

In God alone the noble youth,
Saint Benedict, sought after Truth:
He fled the world's alluring sham
To share the triumph of the Lamb.

O blessed Saint, behold us here
Amid a world of strife and fear;
Detach our hearts from things below
That God may higher gifts bestow.

Most blessed, holy Trinity,
To you be praise eternally,
Your love divine you did impart
Unto our saint's enraptured heart.

ANTIPHON: The man of God, Benedict, forsook the glory of the world, for the Spirit of God was in him.

PSALM 14. *God's Household.*[1]

Who is it that shall dwell with you? * Shall dwell within your kingdom, Lord? / Shall live upon your holy mount?

All those who keep the laws of God, / observing all of his decrees; * who practice justice in their deeds:

Who seek the truth with honesty; / who slander no one with their tongue; * who harm no one with bad intent; / who cast no slurs nor ill remarks that would their neighbor's name destroy;

Who hold in scorn all sin and vice, / but honor those who fear the Lord; * who keep their oaths and promises, / though this may mean a painful loss;

Who lend their money to the poor / and do not make unjust demands of those who are already poor; * who do not falsely testify, / and who would never take a bribe against the just and innocent.

[1] In this booklet the numerical references to the psalms follow the order given in the official Latin liturgical books of the Roman Catholic Church as published by the Vatican Press, Rome, Italy.

The lives of those who do all this / will always please the Lord our God, * and therefore they shall always live / upon God's holy mount in peace.

ANTIPHON: The man of God, Benedict, forsook the glory of the world, for the Spirit of God was in him.

A READING FROM THE DIALOGS OF ST. GREGORY (II, Prol.).

Born at Norcia, Italy, Benedict was sent to Rome for a liberal arts education. Surrounded by vice and crime of every kind, he decided to withdraw from the very world which he had been preparing himself to enter, for he was afraid that, if he acquired any of its learning, he would be drawn down to eternal ruin. In his desire to please God alone, he turned his back on further studies, gave up his home and inheritance, resolving to embrace the religious life. He took this step, fully aware of his ignorance, and yet he was truly wise, uneducated though he may have been.

R̠.   Thanks be to God.

V̠.   The Lord has led the just through the right ways,
R̠.   And has shown him the kingdom of God.

PRAYER: Let us pray. Mighty God, the source of all perfection, by the gift of your grace, the blessed Benedict left all things that he might dedicate himself more fully to your service for the salvation of the world. May all those, who strive to walk the path of Christian perfection, not go astray, but run without stumbling and be rewarded by you with the gift of eternal life. This we ask of you through Christ our Lord.   R̠. Amen.

PRAYER FOR A HAPPY DEATH

V̠.   Pray for us, holy Father Benedict.
R̠.   That we may obtain the grace of a happy death.

Holy Father Benedict, * blessed by God in grace and in name, * while standing in prayer with your hands raised to heaven, * you most happily yielded your angelic spirit into the hands of your Creator. You promised zealously to defend against the snares of the enemy, * in the last struggle of death, * those who shall daily remind you * of your glorious departure and your heavenly joys. Protect us therefore   * this day and every day by your holy blessing, * that we may never be separated from our blessed Lord, * from the company of yourself and of all the blessed. We ask this through Christ our Lord. Amen.

REFLECTIONS ON THE CHRISTIAN WAY OF LIFE

The resolution to strive after Christian perfection is often frustrated by the suggestions of the evil one, or by worldly desires, or by selfish pride. These dissipate our momentary fervor and leave us less advanced than we were before. In fact, having lost a battle or missed an opportunity to advance, we are worse off than before.

I. OBEDIENCE.

St. Benedict teaches us to surround ourselves with a well guarded wall of unworldiness and self-discipline. The school of the Lord's service which he established for his disciples is based on the law of obedience, of an habitual docility to the Master's will.

II. RULE OF LIFE.

For the monk, the will of God is clearly revealed in the precepts of the Rule, in the commands of the superiors, and in the regular observance, all of which he vowed to keep. For Christians in the world, the Commandments of God and of the Church are basic norms for holy living. However, that they may not so easily turn aside from these precepts of a godly life, they will do well to adopt a rule of life, a program of Christian perfection suitable to their state, by which they will be directed and safeguarded and spurred on to persevere on the rugged path that leads to heaven.

III. CHARITY.

The Rule of St. Benedict suggests a simple way of life for all, by stressing (1) that in all things we should seek God and His glory; (2) that we show filial reverence for God by our obedience to lawful authority in all that is morally good; (3) that out of love for Christ we are not to prefer ourselves to others. All of this is summed up in the two great commandments: "You shall love the Lord your God with all your heart, and with all your soul, and with all your mind, and with all your strength; and you shall love your neighbor as yourself" (Mark 12:30-31).

Third Day

THE FATHER

Eternal Father, God of love,
Look kindly on us from above,
And grant that we may never stray
From paths marked out by you each day.

You sent Saint Benedict to be
Our father, who would help us see
How we should daily live aright,
That we might share your vision bright.

To you be praise eternally,
Most blessed, holy Trinity,
Whose loving grace did strength impart
And filled our Saint's enraptured heart.

ANTIPHON: I will make you a great nation, and will bless
you; and you shall be blessed.

PSALM 22. *The Lord Is My Shepherd.*

My shepherd is the Lord, my God, / with him I shall not
ever want; * his verdant pastures give repose; / he leads me
to the running streams, / where I may rest, my soul refresh.

He guides and leads me on right paths, * and, as a loving
shepherd should, / he guards and watches over me;

If I should walk on darksome paths / and in the sombre
shades of death, * no threatening evil need I fear, / for you
are at my side, O Lord, / your rod and staff, they comfort me.

A banquet you prepare for me within the sight of all my
foes, / your table spread as for a guest; * you pour sweet
ointments on my head, / the cup you give me overflows;

Your loving kindness follows me / through all my days
of life on earth; * may I then dwell within your house / for
years to come, for ever, Lord.

ANTIPHON: I will make you a great nation, and will bless
you; and you shall be blessed.

A READING FROM THE RULE OF ST. BENEDICT
(ch. 2).

In his guidance of souls, the abbot should always observe the procedure set forth by the Apostle, who says: "Reprove, entreat, rebuke" (2 Tim. 4:2). Mingling gentleness with severity, according to the circumstances, let him show the rigor of a master and the loving affection of a father; that is, he should more severely reprove the undisciplined and restless, but encourage the obedient, meek, and patient to make still greater progress in virtue; and we charge him to rebuke and punish the negligent and haughty.

℞. **Thanks be to God.**

℣. **You have been pleasing in the sight of the Lord.**

℞. **Therefore the Lord has clothed you with splendor.**

PRAYER: Let us pray. God, our Father, may St. Benedict be our special patron in heaven so that what we cannot achieve by our own strength and merit, we may obtain through his merits and prayers and your loving grace. This we ask of you through Christ our Lord. ℞. Amen.

PRAYER FOR A HAPPY DEATH

℣. **Pray for us, holy Father Benedict.**

℞. **That we may obtain the grace of a happy death.**

Holy Father Benedict, * blessed by God in grace and in name, * while standing in prayer with your hands raised to heaven, * you most happily yielded your angelic spirit into the hands of your Creator. You promised zealously to defend against the snares of the enemy, * in the last struggle of death, * those who shall daily remind you * of your glorious departure and your heavenly joys. Protect us therefore * this day and every day by your holy blessing, * that we may never be separated from our blessed Lord, * from the company of yourself and of all the blessed. We ask this through Christ our Lord. Amen.

REFLECTIONS ON GOD OUR FATHER

In our daily life we are easily distracted from thoughts of God and often find our thoughts centered on ourselves. No wonder that St. Benedict preferred community life, so that monks could live together in prayer and work, under an abbot or spiritual father who is accepted as representing God and "holds the place of Christ" in the monastery.

I.   OUR FATHER WHO ART IN HEAVEN.

Our Lord and Savior has taught us to pray daily: "Our Father who art in heaven." It is this mindfulness of our filial relation to our heavenly Father that gives proper direction and value to our lives. Lack of a supernatural outlook during much of the day leaves our lives empty and almost un-Christian. The spirit of the early Church, so well reflected in St. Benedict's Rule, fostered a deep awareness of membership in the spiritual kingdom on earth, of which Christ is the Head.

II.   OUR SPIRITUAL GUIDE.

We can regain this consciousness of membership in Christ by seeing Christ's authority and the loving care of our heavenly Father exercised in our behalf by those who serve us as spiritual guides and counsellors, especially our confessors and religious superiors, as well as others appointed to assist in the pastoral ministry of the Church. They are our "fathers" and "mothers" in Christ. With St. Paul we say: "I bow my knees before the Father, from whom every family in heaven and on earth is named" (Eph. 3:14).

III.   SPIRITUAL GUIDANCE.

In filial dependence on our heavenly Father we will seek the counsel and guidance of His representatives, our spiritual guides in this life. We can do this by paying closer attention to the ordinary instructions given by them, or by consulting them privately when we need direction in matters concerning our spiritual life. We have been made children of God "by adoption" (Rom. 8:15). This spirit of adopted children of God, infused into us at baptism, will strengthen in us the bond of charity through our common union in Christ under the one Father in heaven.

Fourth Day

THE LAWGIVER

As once upon Cassino's heights,
Our blessed Father still invites
Stout hearts to his monastic school
To live according to his Rule.

Discreet, yet firm, this sacred norm
Of Christian life, may it reform
Our stubborn wills, as we each day
Sincerely strive to walk God's way.

All praise to God the Father be,
And to His Son eternally,
With equal glory, as is meet,
To God the holy Paraclete.

ANTIPHON: A wise man's teaching is a fountain of life.

PSALM 18:8-12. *The Law of God.*

Your laws, O Lord, are perfect, / they give us life and comfort; * your wise decrees are truthful, / they guide the poor and humble;

Your precepts, Lord, are righteous, / they make hearts glad and joyful; * and your commands are faultless, / they take away our blindness;

Your words, O Lord, are holy, / they promise life for ever; * your judgments, Lord, are truthful, / are based on love and justice;

Above all gold more precious / than any finest metal, * and sweeter than the honey / from honeycomb extracted.

A great reward you promise * for those who keep your precepts.

ANTIPHON: A wise man's teaching is a fountain of life.

A READING FROM THE DIALOGS OF ST. GREGORY
(II, Prol.).

I would like to tell you much more about the saintly abbot Benedict. But, there is one point in particular that I would call to your attention. While the man of God was renowned for the many miracles he wrought, he was no less outstanding for the wisdom of his teaching. He wrote a Rule for Monks that is remarkable for its good sense and discretion, as also for its clearness of language. Anyone who wishes to know more about his life and character can discover in his Rule exactly what he was like as an abbot, for his life could not have differed from his teaching.

℟. Thanks be to God.

℣. Those who keep God's law.
℟. Shall dwell in peace.

PRAYER: Let us pray. God our Creator and supreme Legislator, you inspired St. Benedict to compose a Christ-like rule of life, with the Gospel as his guide. Grant that we, who seek to serve you under the guidance of his Rule, may persevere to the end in keeping your commandments. This we ask of you through Christ our Lord.   ℟. Amen.

PRAYER FOR A HAPPY DEATH

℣. Pray for us, holy Father Benedict.
℟. That we may obtain the grace of a happy death.

Holy Father Benedict, * blessed by God in grace and in name, * while standing in prayer with your hands raised to heaven, * you most happily yielded your angelic spirit into the hands of your Creator. You promised zealously to defend against the snares of the enemy, * in the last struggle of death, * those who shall daily remind you * of your glorious departure and your heavenly joys. Protect us therefore * this day and every day by your holy blessing, * that we may never be separated from our blessed Lord, * from the company of yourself and of all the blessed. We ask this through Christ our Lord.   Amen.

REFLECTIONS ON THE LAW OF GOD

"Not everyone who says to me, 'Lord, Lord,' shall enter the kingdom of heaven, but only those who do the will of my heavenly Father" (Matthew 7:21). Too readily we imagine ourselves good Catholics when, with sincere intention and good will, we do what we think is right, although we actually transgress the law of God in many ways by following our own misguided judgment.

I. VALUE OF THE LAW.

St. Bernard warns us that "he who has himself as a master, makes himself the disciple of a fool." Since spiritual perfection consists in conforming our will to God's will, we must aim to know God's good pleasure, saying with the Psalmist: "Your laws are far more precious than a thousand gold and silver coins; they give me greater joy and peace than all the riches in the world" (Ps. 118:72).

II. RESPECT FOR AUTHORITY.

Keeping the Commandments is not possible without a deep sense of respect for legitimate authority. If we look upon our superiors as God's representatives, we shall seek His law from their mouth and be guided safely in the way of obedience. The prophet Malachias said of the Old Testament priest: "for the lips of a priest should guard knowledge, and the people should seek instruction from his mouth, for he is the messenger of the Lord of hosts" (Mal. 2:7). With all the more reason do we turn to Christ's anointed priests for the law of life.

III. BEHOLD THE LAW!

In writing his Rule, St. Benedict was moved by the conviction that nothing matters so much in the spiritual life as obedience to God's holy will. Therefore he undertook to summarize the Gospel precepts, and he offers them to his followers with the words: "Behold the law under which you wish to do battle. If you can keep it, enter; if not, then freely depart" (ch. 58). Indeed, in life's struggle the knowledge of the divine will is a constant source of courage and consolation. "Your laws, O Lord, are perfect, they give us life and comfort; your wise decrees are truthful, they guide the poor and humble; your precepts, Lord, are righteous, they make hearts glad and joyful" (Ps. 18-8-9).

Fifth Day

THE MIRACLE WORKER

With sign of Cross, your weapon bright,
You put the evil one to flight.
Protect us by your loving care,
Defend us from the tempter's snare.

They offered you some poisoned wine,
But you then made the sacred sign:
The cup of death broke open wide,
For death could not with life abide.

To you be praise eternally,
Most blessed, holy Trinity,
Whose loving grace did strength impart
And filled our Saint's enraptured heart.

ANTIPHON: No one can work these signs, unless God be
              with him.

PSALM 95:1-6. *The Greatness of God.*

Sing a new and joyful song, * praise the Lord in psalms
and hymns, / all you peoples of the earth.

Sing to him and bless his name, / his salvation loud proclaim, / day by day proclaim his name; * spread his name
throughout the world, / make it known in pagan lands, /
tell them of God's wondrous works.

God is great, a mighty Lord, / worthy of all praise and
thanks; * clothed in awesome majesty, / far above all other
gods.

Pagan gods are lifeless things, / vain and useless works
of man, / powerless to speak or act; * but our God is strong
and great, / he it is who gave us life, / he it is who made all
things, / all the oceans, earth, and skies;

Clothed in splendid majesty, / God displays his might
and power * in his holy dwelling place.

ANTIPHON: No one can work these signs, unless God be
              with him.

A READING FROM THE DIALOGS OF ST. GREGORY (II, Prol.).

Those who are in close union with God may, if necessity requires, accomplish marvelous things, sometimes by prayer, sometimes by a power given to them. St. John says: "But to all who received him, who believed in his name, he gave power to become children of God" (John 1:12). Should we then be surprised if those who are children of God use this power to work signs and wonders?

R̂.   **Thanks be to God.**

V̂.   **He was filled with the spirit of God.**
R̂.   **He worked wonders by the power of God.**

PRAYER: Let us pray. God of power and might, you have shown forth your goodness by the many miracles which you wrought through your holy servant Benedict. Grant us the final grace of eternal blessedness. This we ask of you through Christ our Lord.   R̂. Amen.

PRAYER FOR A HAPPY DEATH

V̂.   Pray for us, holy Father Benedict.
R̂.   That we may obtain the grace of a happy death.

Holy Father Benedict, * blessed by God in grace and in name, * while standing in prayer with your hands raised to heaven, * you most happily yielded your angelic spirit into the hands of your Creator. You promised zealously to defend against the snares of the enemy, * in the last struggle of death, * those who shall daily remind you * of your glorious departure and your heavenly joys. Protect us therefore * this day and every day by your holy blessing, * that we may never be separated from our blessed Lord, * from the company of yourself and of all the blessed. We ask this through Christ our Lord.   Amen.

REFLECTIONS ON THE POWER OF GOD

Many people scoff at miracles, because they are so far from that inner life with God which brings heaven close to earth and makes heavenly powers visible. Of course, miracles still do happen in the lives of God's saints, but more rarely. Is it that saints are become more rare?

I.   BY THE POWER OF GOD.

God's arm is not limited in its power. His almighty will still rules the universe. In His own designs God at times still shows His miraculous power, not to satisfy a Herod's curiosity "hoping to see some miracle" (Luke 23:8), but that the faith of believers be strengthened and the name of God be glorified. "This, the first of his miracles, Jesus did at Cana in Galilee, and manifested his glory, and his disciples believed in him" (John 2:11).

II.   FOR GOD'S GLORY.

Before holy men or women are beatified or canonized as saints, it must be established that one or more miracles were wrought through their intercession. Is it not to show that God glorified His servants? Indeed, it manifests divine approval, and yet the power of miracles is rather a confirmation of the faithful service of the saints for God's glory, whereby they merited also a share in heavenly glory. "How can one who is a sinner do such miracles?" (John 9:16).

III.   BY THE WILL OF GOD.

What really endows the saints with the power of miracles is their absolute faith in God and complete abandonment to the divine will. They will and desire all things from God's own viewpoint, and in this perfect union of wills the omnipotent divine will seems to yield more freely to man's will altogether absorbed in God. Thus where faith enlightens the saints to see God's will in everything, and hope gives them assurance of extraordinary help, it is their great charity that exercises a power beyond all human strength. St. Gregory's life of St. Benedict bears eloquent witness to this.

Sixth Day

THE PROPHET

O favored Saint, in vision bright,
In God's transcending, wondrous light,
You saw the world in one bright ray,
The universe before you lay.

Obtain for us a vision clear
And save us from all human fear,
That by your guidance we may reach
Perfection's goal which you did teach.

To you be praise eternally,
Most blessed, holy Trinity,
Whose loving grace did strength impart
And filled our Saint's enraptured heart.

ANTIPHON: By the light of contemplation his spirit was
lifted heavenward.

CANTICLE OF ZACHARY (Luke 1:68-75). *Promise of Salvation.*

Blessed be the Lord God of Israel, * for he has visited
and redeemed his people;
And has raised up a horn of salvation for us, * in the
house of David his servant,
As he spoke by the mouth of his holy prophets from of
old, * that we shall be saved from our enemies, / and from
the hand of all who hate us:
To perform the mercy promised to our fathers, * and to
remember his holy covenant, / the oath which he swore to
our father Abraham:
To grant us that we, being delivered from the hand of
our enemies, * might serve him without fear,
In holiness and righteousness before him, * all the days
of our life.

ANTIPHON: By the light of contemplation his spirit was
lifted heavenward.

A READING FROM THE DIALOGS OF ST. GREGORY (II, Prol.).

Long before the night office began, the man of God Benedict was standing at his window, where he watched and prayed while the rest were still asleep. In the dead of night he suddenly saw a flood of light shining down from above, more brilliant than the sun, and with it every trace of darkness cleared away. He saw the whole world gathered up before his eyes in what appeared to be a single ray of light. Absorbed as he was in God, it was now easy for him to see all that lay beneath God. In the light outside that was shining before his eyes, there was a brightness which reached into his mind and lifted his spirit heavenward, showing him the insignificance of all that lies below.

℞.   Thanks be to God.

℣.   The heart of the wise man.
℞.   Will know the time and the way.

PRAYER: Let us pray. All-seeing and all-knowing God, grant us the gift of holy contemplation, so that we may see and understand life on this earth as you see it, and as St. Benedict describes it in his Rule for all who seek God. This we ask of you through Christ our Lord.   ℞. Amen.

PRAYER FOR A HAPPY DEATH

℣.   Pray for us, holy Father Benedict.
℞.   That we may obtain the grace of a happy death.

Holy Father Benedict, * blessed by God in grace and in name, * while standing in prayer with your hands raised to heaven, * you most happily yielded your angelic spirit into the hands of your Creator. You promised zealously to defend against the snares of the enemy, * in the last struggle of death, * those who shall daily remind you * of your glorious departure and your heavenly joys. Protect us therefore * this day and every day by your holy blessing, * that we may never be separated from our blessed Lord, * from the company of yourself and of all the blessed. We ask this through Christ our Lord.   Amen.

REFLECTIONS ON THE GIFTS OF GOD

"Make charity your aim, and eagerly desire the spiritual gifts, especially that you may prophesy" (1 Cor. 14:1). When Saint Paul exhorts the Corinthians in these words, he certainly has in mind the good of the community more than individual edification. Such extraordinary spiritual gifts, called charisms, were more common at the Church's beginning.

I. SPIRITUAL GIFTS.

In the life of grace and charity God bestows various special gifts, such as St. Paul enumerates in First Corinthians: utterance of wisdom and of knowledge, the gift of faith, of healing and working of miracles, prophecy, discernment of spirits, the speaking of tongues, and interpretation of tongues (12:4-11). All are for the good of the whole Mystical Body as member serves member unto edification. Chosen souls that even in our day are favored with such gifts have a special mission for the good of the Church.

II. MESSENGERS OF GOD.

St. Benedict's many miracles and his gifts of prophecy and discernment of spirits, of which St. Gregory speaks in Book II of his Dialogs, are credentials of St. Benedict's providential mission in the Church. For all nations and for all times the ideals of his life and teaching were to stand as an approved norm for Christian living, just as the Old Testament prophets had been God's messengers to teach and warn the erring and to console the God-fearing.

III. EYES FOR THE BLIND.

Those ancient seers were eyes for the spiritually blind. They directed the wayward sheep back to ways of salvation and pointed unceasingly to the promised Redeemer. The saintly prophets and spiritual guides in our day warn us also against the dangers strewn in our path and keep us directed in mind and heart to the one thing necessary. "Seek first the kingdom of God and his justice" (Matthew 6:33). "That in all things God may be glorified" (1 Pet. 4:11) was adopted by Saint Benedict to serve as a watchword for all of us (ch. 57).

Seventh Day

THE TEACHER

Beloved Father, we now pray:
Instruct us how to walk God's way,
That we may not reject God's law,
But quickly from all sin withdraw.

Our voices now we gladly raise
To sing the Lord's eternal praise;
This praise of God, as taught by you,
Is rightly God's eternal due.

All praise to God the Father be,
And to His Son eternally,
With equal glory, as is meet,
To God the holy Paraclete.

ANTIPHON: The holy monk Benedict could not have lived
differently from what he taught.

PSALM 33:11-16. *The Teachings of God.*

My children, come near to me now, * and listen to what
I shall say / concerning the fear of the Lord:

Now, which of you truly loves life / and wishes for
happiness here? * If truly you wish to have life / and seek
to enjoy the good things which God has bestowed upon us:

Then keep your tongue from evil speech, / and guard
your lips from telling lies; * stay far away from evil deeds, /
pursue and strive for lasting peace.

The Lord has his eyes on the just, / he listens to pleas
of the just; * the wicked he scorns and rejects, / and every
remembrance of them will be without honor or praise.

ANTIPHON: The holy monk Benedict could not have lived
differently from what he taught.

A READING FROM THE RULE OF ST. BENEDICT
(ch. 2).

When anyone accepts the name of abbot, he should govern his
disciples with a twofold teaching: that is, he should show by his

deeds, even more than by his words, all that is good and holy. To those disciples sufficiently able to understand he will make known the commands of God by word of mouth; but to the hard-hearted and simple-minded he will teach the divine precepts by his deeds.

℞. Thanks be to God.

℣. The mouth of the just utters wisdom.
℞. And his tongue speaks justice.

PRAYER: Let us pray. God of wisdom and of counsel, raise up in your Church the Spirit which guided the man of God, Benedict, so that, filled with that same Holy Spirit, we may seek to love what he loved, and to practice what he taught. This we ask of you through Christ our Lord. ℞. Amen.

PRAYER FOR A HAPPY DEATH

℣. Pray for us, holy Father Benedict.
℞. That we may obtain the grace of a happy death.

Holy Father Benedict, * blessed by God in grace and in name, * while standing in prayer with your hands raised to heaven, * you most happily yielded your angelic spirit into the hands of your Creator. You promised zealously to defend against the snares of the enemy, * in the last struggle of death, * those who shall daily remind you * of your glorious departure and your heavenly joys. Protect us therefore * this day and every day by your holy blessing, * that we may never be separated from our blessed Lord, * from the company of yourself and of all the blessed. We ask this through Christ our Lord. Amen.

REFLECTIONS ON GOD'S TEACHINGS

In the order of Providence we are taught and directed by those whom God places over us. St. Benedict is deeply aware of this divine arrangement and feels himself called to act the part of teacher towards his disciples. In the opening words of the Prolog to his Rule he lays down the conditions for successfully learning the all-important lessons of the spiritual life.

I. LISTEN TO THE PRECEPTS.

God will never violate, by forcing us to do good, the gift of free will with which He endowed us. We must, of our own accord, turn to Him, seek Him, "incline the ear of our heart" to His teaching which is being imparted to us by our legitimate instructors. Therefore our blessed Patriarch warns against forgetfulness and inattentiveness regarding our supernatural goal and the means of attaining it. We must never depart from due filial devotedness to our spiritual guides.

II. CHEERFULLY ACCEPT THE ADMONITIONS.

Those who receive the word of God and the admonitions of His representatives "in a good and honest heart" (Luke 8:15), will bring forth manifold fruit; or in the words of the Holy Rule, "will run the way of God's commandments" (Prolog) and "hasten to their heavenly home" (ch. 73). Away, therefore, with all thoughtlessness, fickleness, and sloth. "Let the hearts of those rejoice who seek the Lord and praise his name" (Ps. 104:3).

III. CARRY THEM OUT FAITHFULLY.

Between the generous resolve and the actual execution of a good work there often intervenes a fatal inertia, disheartening to teacher and pupil alike. The faithful disciples, so says St. Benedict, "will immediately put aside their own tasks, forsaking their own will, disengaging themselves and leaving unfinished what they were doing, and quickly carry out by their deeds, with the ready step of obedience, the word of him who commands. The spoken command of the master is followed so quickly by the finished work of the disciple that the two seem to merge with each other in one and the same moment, with a swiftness prompted by the fear of God and by an ardent desire to advance on the way to eternal life" (ch. 5).

Eighth Day

THE APOSTLE

O Lord, our Life and Truth and Way,
Direct us lest we go astray.
May we with apostolic zeal
Go forth, the wounds of strife to heal.

Lord God, we pray that we may climb
With Benedict to heights sublime;
His rule our guide, its goal our aim:
Return to you from whom we came.

All praise to God the Father be,
To you His Son, eternally,
With equal glory, as is meet,
To God the holy Paraclete.

ANTIPHON: Those who offered him food for his body received in return from his lips the Word of
God, the food of life.

PSALM 18:1-7. *The Good News of God.*

The heavens declare your glory, Lord, * the skies proclaim your handiwork;
The sun gives forth its light to day, / each day pours out
the word to day; * the moon and stars give light to night, /
each night imparts the news to night;
No sound, no speech, no word is heard, / and yet their
voice is clearly heard; * throughout the world their voice
resounds, / proclaims the glory of the Lord, / to farthest
bounds of all the earth.
And in the sky the Lord has set / a tabernacle for the
sun, * which, like a groom in fine array, / or like a giant
in the race, / appearing at the dawn of day, / comes forth
with joy to run its course, / to shed its heat and light on all.
At close of day, its course now run, / far in the west,
with bright display, * into its tent it goes again, / all
through the night to rest again.

ANTIPHON: Those who offered him food for the body received in return from his lips the Word of
God, the food of life.

A READING FROM THE DIALOGS OF ST. GREGORY
(II. Prol.).

When the man of God arrived at the summit of Monte Cassino,
he found an old temple there, dedicated to Apollo, where the people
of the vicinity still carried on their pagan worship, as their ancestors
had done. Going to the temple, the man of God destroyed the statue
of Apollo, overturned the altar, and cut down the trees of the nearby
sacred groves. He then converted the temple of Apollo into a chapel
dedicated to St. Martin of Tours. Where the altar of Apollo had
stood, he built a chapel in honor of St. John the Baptist. Finally, by
his zealous preaching and instruction, he gradually won the people
of the countryside over to the true faith.

R̥.   Thanks be to God.

V̥.   Faith comes from what is heard.
R̥.   And what is heard comes by the preaching of Christ.

PRAYER: Let us pray. Lord God, it is your will that the
whole world look to you for salvation and de-
liverance from the slavery of sin. Grant us a sense of mission,
such as St. Benedict had, and fill us with an apostolic spirit
that we may, by the example of our life, help to draw others
to you. This we ask of you through Christ our Lord.   R̥. Amen.

PRAYER FOR A HAPPY DEATH

V̥.   Pray for us, holy Father Benedict.
R̥.   That we may obtain the grace of a happy death.

Holy Father Benedict, * blessed by God in grace and in
name, * while standing in prayer with your hands raised to
heaven, * you most happily yielded your angelic spirit into
the hands of your Creator. You promised zealously to defend
against the snares of the enemy, * in the last struggle of
death, * those who shall daily remind you * of your glorious
departure and your heavenly joys. Protect us therefore *
this day and every day by your holy blessing, * that we may
never be separated from our blessed Lord, * from the com-

pany of yourself and of all the blessed. We ask this through Christ our Lord. Amen.

REFLECTIONS ON LOVE OF GOD AND NEIGHBOR

The life of perfection, growth in charity, will inevitably blossom forth in holy zeal for God and neighbor. The apostle is characterized by a zealous spirit, whether chosen for a special mission to spread the kingdom of God, or to serve the Master in the more ordinary and wider sense of seeking to make God loved and served.

I. CHARITY REACHES OUT TO OTHERS.

Zeal is love aflame. Those who reach a certain degree of charity by overcoming self-love will naturally be more concerned about the good of others. They find in God their life and love, and find their neighbor in God's embrace, and learn to love others more and more. "Let us not love in word or speech, but in deed and in truth" (1 John 3:18).

II. CHARITY EMBRACES ALL.

What St. Benedict says about a virtuous zeal applies here. "This is the zeal which monks should exercise with the most fervent charity. They will therefore show esteem for each other with all due honor and respect. They will, with the greatest patience, bear with one another's weaknesses, whether bodily infirmities or faults of character. They will seek to surpass each other in obedience one to another. Nor will anyone follow what seems only good for himself, but rather do what is good for another" (ch. 72).

III. CHARITY IS ENDURING.

True love, built up on humility and rooted in God, will never fail. This is the love of which St. Benedict speaks when he says that "true love of God, when perfect, casts out fear" (ch. 7). Nothing can daunt such a love, because when we have reached this stage in the spiritual life, we are no longer impeded by self-interest or shaken by fear. We can exclaim with St. Paul: "Who shall separate us from the love of Christ? Shall tribulation, or distress, or persecution? . . . . No, in all these things we are more than conquerors, through him who loved us" (Rom. 8:35-37).

Ninth Day

THE MAN OF GOD

With Gospel teachings as your guide
You wrote a rule that would provide
A way of life for all who aim
To follow Christ, His Name proclaim.

While yet on earth, your fame spread wide;
As man of God, you could not hide.
We humbly beg to share the joy
That now is yours without alloy.

To you be praise eternally,
Most blessed, holy Trinity,
Whose loving grace did strength impart
And filled our Saint's enraptured heart.

ANTIPHON: Let us rejoice in the Lord, celebrating the
             memory of the holy abbot Benedict.

PSALM 8. *God's Majesty and Man's Dignity.*

O Lord, how wonderful your name! / How great your
name throughout the world! * How splendid is your majesty! / More splendid than the earth and sky.

The mouths of infants praising you / confound and
silence all your foes, * and shame all those who seek revenge.

I marvel at the earth and sky, / the sun and moon and
all the stars, / the wondrous works of your own hands; *
you made them all, O Lord, our God.

And yet, midst all your wondrous works, / it was on us
you set your mind; * but why should you thus favor us? /
Why should you even think of us? / Why should you even
care for us? / For, what is mortal man to you?

With glory you created us, / you crowned us with great
dignity, * a little less than angels, Lord.

You set us over all your works, / you gave us all the
earth to rule, / and placed all creatures under us, / the
creatures of your loving hands: * the sheep and oxen, beasts
and birds, / whatever walks or crawls or flies, / whatever
swims the ocean paths.

O Lord, our God, how wonderful, * how great your name throughout the world.

ANTIPHON: Let us rejoice in the Lord, celebrating the memory of the holy abbot Benedict.

A READING FROM THE GOSPEL OF ST. MATTHEW (19:27-29).

Then Peter said to Jesus: "Lo, we have left everything and followed you. What then shall we have?" Jesus said to them: "Truly I say to you, in the new world, when the Son of man shall sit on his glorious throne, you who have followed me will also sit on twelve thrones, judging the twelve tribes of Israel. And everyone who has left houses or brothers or sisters or father or mother or children or lands, for my name s sake, will receive a hundredfold, and inherit eternal life."

R. Thanks be to God.

V. The Lord has loved him and clothed him with splendor.

R. He has clothed him with a robe of glory.

PRAYER: Let us pray. Almighty and everlasting God, you freed the man of God, Benedict, from the prison of the flesh and bore him up to heaven to enjoy the vision of your glory. Grant us, through his merits, the spirit of penance, forgiveness of our sins, so that we may one day share the joys of eternal life with him and all the saints. This we ask of you through Christ our Lord.   R. Amen.

PRAYER FOR A HAPPY DEATH

V. Pray for us, holy Father Benedict.

R. That we may obtain the grace of a happy death.

Holy Father Benedict, * blessed by God in grace and in name, * while standing in prayer with your hands raised to heaven, * you most happily yielded your angelic spirit into the hands of your Creator. You promised zealously to defend against the snares of the enemy, * in the last struggle of death, * those who shall daily remind you * of your glorious departure and your heavenly joys. Protect us therefore * this day and every day by your holy blessing, * that we may never be separated from our blessed Lord, * from the company of yourself and of all the blessed. We ask this through Christ our Lord.   Amen.

REFLECTIONS ON ETERNAL LIFE IN HEAVEN

The "unfading crown of glory" (1 Peter 5:4) which has been reserved for the just is the reward of perfect charity. The faithful servant who has overcome all inordinate affections and is filled with the love of God is ready for the blissful life of heaven, where nothing can ever turn him away from the blessed vision of God.

I.   PROMISE OF GLORY.

In the lives of the early Christians the thought of heaven was ever present to encourage and console them amid their daily trials. The same truth and expectation has spurred on the men of God in all ages, because of the promise of final victory in Christ. With the same assurance St. Benedict tells his sons "to desire eternal life with all spiritual longing" (ch. 4).

II.   HOPE IN THE PROMISE.

To keep this yearning alive in mind and heart must be our daily resolve so that, as St. Benedict reminds us, "we may be worthy to enjoy the vision of God who has called us to His kingdom" (Prolog). If we place our trust in Christ and prefer nothing whatsoever to Him, then surely will He "bring us all together in life everlasting" (ch. 72).

III.   PERSEVERANCE.

The consoling words of Saint James should, therefore, ring constantly in our ears to incite us to perseverance: "Blessed is the man who endures trial; for when he has stood the test, he shall receive the crown of life, which God has promised to those who love him" (James 1:12). Also we should often recall that ardent appeal of St. Benedict: "Let us never depart from under His guidance, but persevere in the monastery until death, in the observance of His teachings, so that, by our patience, we may share in the sufferings of Christ, and thus deserve to share in His kingdom" (Prolog).

Hymn to St. Benedict

The first of the two melodies suggested for the opening hymn on each day of the Novena is an old chant formerly used for the Latin hymn, "Signifer Invictissime," which was sung at Matins on July 11, the feast of the Solemnity of St. Benedict. For many years the hymn and melody have been sung daily by the monks of Monte Cassino, gathered together at the tomb of Sts. Benedict and Scholastica after the noonday meal.

1. The gold - en sun lights up the east Re - calls, by
2. O gra - cious fa - ther, on this day With hum - ble
3. All praise to God the Fa - ther be, And to His

1. sol - emn year - ly feast, When Ben - e - dict as - cend-
2. hearts and words we pray, That, taught by you to live
3. Son, e - ter - nal - ly, With e - qual glo - ry, as

1. ed high To heav - en's man - sions in the sky.
2. a - right, We may en - joy God's vi - sion bright.
3. is meet, To God the ho - ly Par - a - clete.

Hymn to St. Benedict

Alternate Melody

1. The gold - en sun lights up the east Re - calls, by
2. O gra - cious fa - ther, on this day With hum - ble
3. All praise to God the Fa - ther be, And to His

1. sol - emn year - ly feast, When Ben - e - dict as - cend-
2. hearts and words we pray, That, taught by you to live
3. Son, e - ter - nal - ly, With e - qual glo - ry, as

1. ed high To heav - en's man - sions in the sky.
2. a - right, We may en - joy God's vi - sion bright.
3. is meet, To God the ho - ly Par - a - clete.